ENOUGH OF FRANKIE ALREADY!

Written by Felicia Capers

Illustrated by Christopher Fabor Muhammad

Miracle's Tasty Express and Advertising LLC
(786) 999-3947
Miraclestastyexpress2014@gmail.com

COOKIES CRAYONS & KIDS MEDIA LLC

NEW JERSEY, USA

Copyright © Felicia Capers 2013 (Text)
Copyright © Christopher Fabor Muhammad 2013 (Illustrations)

ALL RIGHTS RESERVED.

No part of this publication may be reproduced, stored in a retrieval system, or transmitted in any form or by any means, electronic, mechanical, photocopying, recording or otherwise without written permission of the publisher or author. This is a work of fiction. Names, characters, places and incidents either are products of the author's imagination or are used fictitiously. Any resemblance to actual events or locales or persons, living or dead, is entirely coincidental.

Enough of Frankie Already!
Third Edition

ISBN-13: 978-0-9895054-2-0

Library of Congress Control Number: 2013910803
JUV039230 JUVENILE FICTION / Social Issues / Bullying
Onix Audience code JUV-04

Published by Cookies, Crayons & Kids Media, LLC, a division of Posh Publishing, LLC

www.frankiethebully.com

For Taylor and Tyson-
Reach for the stars. When it gets tough,
PUSH HARDER! I always got your back.

FC

For All Our Youth who I have with a Passion served in the Past,
Present and will continue to do so in the Future!
Proceed with Reason and Purpose!

CFM

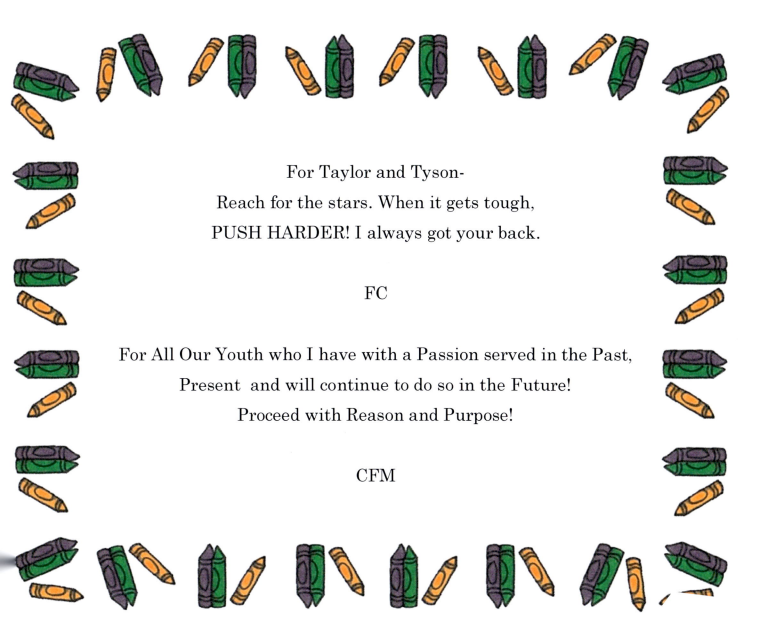

You see, my name is Amir and if you were a student at Jefferson Elementary like me, then you would know how I feel. You would know how we all feel around here. You would also get to know Frankie *really* well.

Frankie is in third grade and I am in second grade.

He is the biggest bully you ever would know.

Every day we see Frankie at school. We see him on the playground.

We even see him after school with his silly baseball cap on his silly head.

He always has a big silly smile on his big silly face!

I cannot tell you why he does the things he does to us but I know that we have all had enough. At the beginning of the school year, Frankie cornered my friend Christopher in the hallway on his way to the bathroom. He stole Christopher's hall pass and flushed it down the toilet.

One time, Frankie walked right up to my friend Marcus, grabbed his notebook...

...and ripped the pages out, right there in front of all of us.

I wish I had enough time to tell you about all of the evil things Frankie has done to me. Just last month, he pushed me down at recess and put his foot on my back while my face was buried in the dirt.

He told me that my braids were too neat and shiny and needed a little dust. Can you believe that?

Frankie even ripped the buttons off my clean white shirt on picture day last week. I sure hope mama does not notice the missing buttons when the pictures come back.

Today, after class was dismissed, I was sure that I would get out of the building before Frankie saw me.

It seems I was too slow. He caught me sneaking out of Mr. Wilson's art room.

Frankie threw my book bag up against the door and all of my math homework went flying everywhere. Now can you see why I am so mad? Frankie has got to be stopped!

"Amir." Marcus ran over to help me. "I saw what Frankie did to you. What are we going to do about him?"

"I am too angry to think about Frankie. I don't even want to talk about him!" I snapped at Marcus. "Look at my homework! It's a mess!"

"Hey!" I yelled, getting up from the hard concrete. "What is your problem Frankie?"

"Keep quiet short stuff! You second graders are nothing but babies. All of you!" Frankie shouted back at me.

I took a deep breath. I knew it was now or never. "So that's why you are such a big old bully, huh? You pick on us because we are second graders? How would you like it if someone bigger than you picked on you Frankie?"

Then my friend Alesha said, "Frankie! Picking on smaller kids does not make you tough!"

"None of you know me! None of you know what it is like when the fifth graders pick on me," Frankie yelled back at us. "No one sees what the eighth graders do to them. Everyone gets bullied at this school."

"Just because the fifth graders bully you, does not mean you can bully us," I told Frankie.

"You should not bully someone just because they are younger than you," Alesha told him. Just then Mr. Wilson came over and asked, "What's going on here?"

"The fifth graders have been bullying Frankie," Alesha said.

"That's awful." Mr. Wilson turned to Frankie. "How long has this been going on?"

Frankie did not answer. He only shrugged his shoulders and pointed across the playground where the fifth graders played football.

When Mr. Wilson looked across the playground, he could not believe what he saw. While some fifth graders tried to play football, the eighth graders stole their ball. In every corner of the playground, Mr. Wilson saw Jefferson Elementary students being bullied by each other.

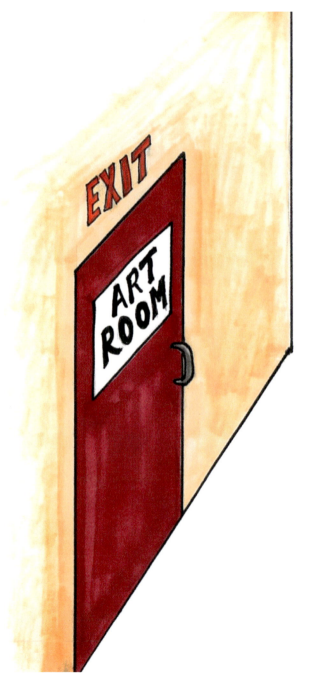

Suddenly, I had an idea. It was time that we sent a message that no bullying would be allowed at Jefferson Elementary.

I asked Mr. Wilson if we could spend the rest of recess inside his art room and I gave him a list of supplies that we would need.

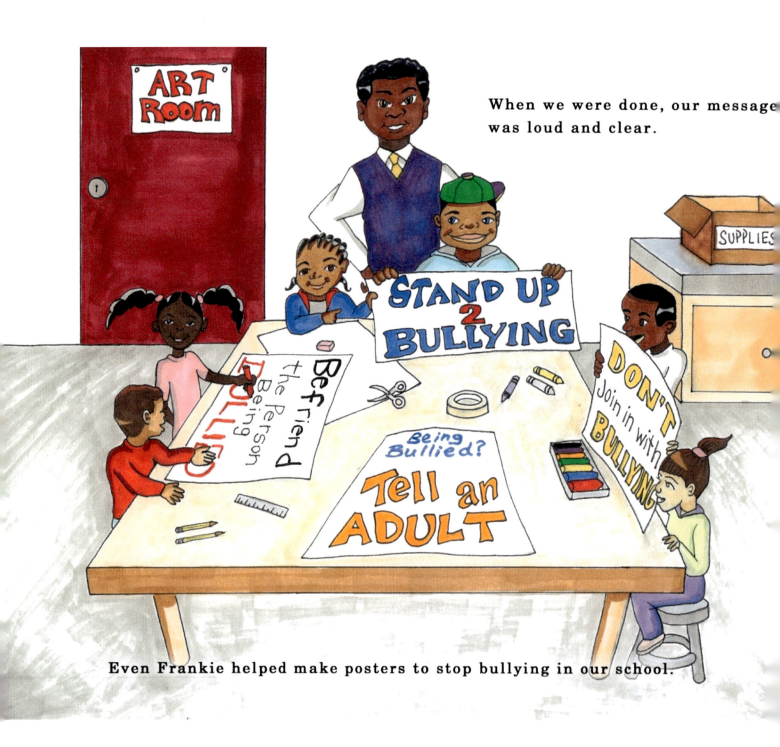

When we were done, our message was loud and clear.

Even Frankie helped make posters to stop bullying in our school.

Mr. Wilson said we had started a new project for our whole school. We call it The Enough Already Campaign Against Bullying.

"It does not matter if you are tall or short," Mr. Wilson told us.

"It does not matter if you are younger or older, no one should be bullied at this school because they are different from someone else."

"I am very proud of all of you today. These posters will hang in the hallways for a very long time at Jefferson Elementary, a bully-free school."

DISCUSSION GUIDE

1. How do you think the other students at Jefferson Elementary will feel about the new posters about bullying that are now hanging in their school?

2. Instead of bullying students who are younger than you, how can you help them? How does your school allow you to help students in your school that are younger than you?

3. What are some other ways Amir and his friends can stop bullying at their school?

4. If you saw a bully bullying your friend, what would you do?

5. Amir was angry and annoyed at the beginning of the story. What are some things that make you angry and annoy you?

6. When you are angry, how do you calm down? Who do you talk to?

7. What is respect?

8. How can you show respect to your classmates, to your teachers, to your school, to your family, to your community?

ABOUT THE AUTHOR

Felicia Capers, Founder of Posh Publishing, LLC, author, publisher, and workshop leader, resides in New Jersey. Felicia has championed children's issues for nearly a decade and serves on an HIB (Harassment Intimidation Bullying) advisory board for a large New Jersey school district. The children's division of Posh Publishing, LLC- Cookies, Crayons & Kids Media, has three objectives: 1) to promote literacy; 2) to celebrate the minds of young thinkers; 3) to empower youth to engage civically. Felicia enjoys traveling, dancing, and spending time with her two children.

ABOUT THE ILLUSTRATOR

Christopher Fabor Muhammad, Founder of Creative Force Inc., educator and artist, resides in New Jersey. Chris believes arts in education is not a choice but a necessary infusion for student success. In his afterschool program, Creative Force Alliance for Education through Arts & Culture, Chris provides instruction and expressions in visual art, theatrical art, creative writing, music and more. Medium used for *Enough of Frankie Already!* is copic markers on vellum.

Made in the USA
Columbia, SC
02 April 2019